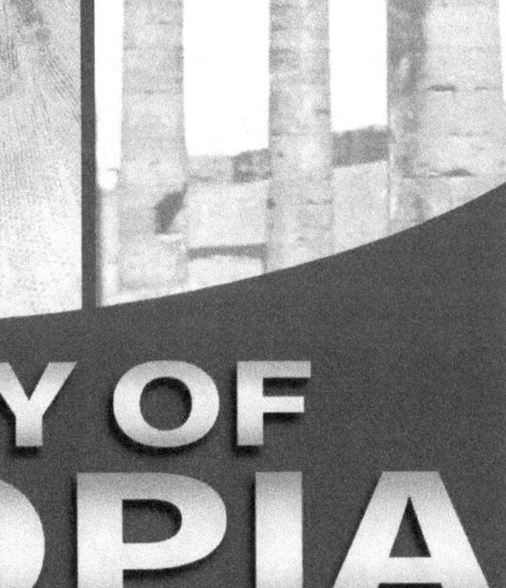

HISTORY OF ETHIOPIA

A BRIEF HISTORY FROM BEGINNING TO END

HISTORY HUB

Bonus Downloads

Every purchase comes with a FREE download!

History of Ethiopia

A Brief History from Beginning to the End

History Shorts

CONTENTS

Chapter One: Introduction

Chapter Two: Ancient Hominids, Husbandry, Language and Relics

Chapter Three: Links to Ancient Egypt and Greece

Chapter Four: Ethiopia's Rulers

Chapter Five: The Rise of Ethiopia During Menelik I's Reign

Chapter Six: The Rise of Ethiopia During the Reign of Menelik II

Chapter Seven: The Rise of Ethiopia During Haile Selassie's Reign

Chapter Eight: The Fall of Ethiopia During Menelik I's Reign

Chapter Nine: The Fall of Ethiopia During the Reign of Menelik II

Chapter Ten: The Fall of Ethiopia During Haile Selassie's Reign

Chapter Eleven: The Aftermath of the Fall of Ethiopia

Chapter Twelve: Conclusion

Chapter Thirteen: Discussion Question

Chapter Fourteen: Quiz Question

Your Free Bonus Download

Chapter One

Introduction

Ethiopia is more than just another beautiful East African country. It's a melting pot of cultures, languages, timekeeping, cuisine, trade, and tourism that has evolved since its establishment in the thirteenth century. Unlike some of its African and international counterparts, Ethiopia has a rich history of powerful female rulers. In fact, as recently as 1916 to 1930, Empress and Queen Zewditu ruled the country, and was the first globally recognized female African head of state. Being a progressive country did not stop there for Ethiopia—a Jewish Queen, Gudit, ruled parts of the country in the 10th century. While Gudit's short-lived reign ended in throngs of fire, it cannot be denied that Ethiopia is a trailblazing country. Its main claim to fame is that it is one of only two African countries (the other being Liberia) which have never been colonized. Many parties have tried to bend Ethiopia and its residents to their will over the centuries and have failed. An attempted Italian occupation failed to hold sway over the country between 1936 and 1941.

The vibrant country runs on its own calendar. Instead of the solar calendar that the rest of the world has adopted from Ancient Rome, Ethiopia follows a 13-month calendar. The Ethiopian calendar is derived from the country's Egyptian origins and includes leap years every four years. This means that they are currently living through the year 2012! We hope they'll have a better 2020 than the rest of the world did.

Modern mankind has Ethiopia's history to thank for its favorite drink: coffee! A legend passed down through history, from generation to generation, is that a sheep herder noticed that his goats were more energetic and unable to sleep at night after feasting on a particular berry during the day. He used the berries to make his own brew and felt that he could stay awake during his long night shifts after drinking it. He shared this brew with local monks and the rest is caffeinated history! Today, thanks to this delicious part of Ethiopia's remarkable history, 500 billion cups of coffee are drunk every year.

Religion and economy are two of Ethiopia's mainstays. Its economy had evolved from a rudimentary barter system that existed for centuries before the Aksumite king Menelik II established the first bank in the country, the Bank of Abyssinia, in 1905. With branches in Harar, Dire

Dawa, Gore, and Dembidolo, the bank was renamed as the Bank of Ethiopia in 1932.

Ethiopia's history is steeped in an ancient form of Christianity. This Orthodox form of faith means that to this day, Ethiopians do not eat meat on Wednesdays and Fridays. This makes the country a perfect vacation spot for vegetarians as Ethiopia's cuisine features plenty of vegetable-based curries, stews, and dishes.

Adding to the historical influences the Christian faith has had on Ethiopia, the country is believed to be home to the biblical Ark of The Covenant which holds the Ten Commandments. St. Mary of Tsion, known as "The Mother Church of Ethiopia" employs a special guardian for the Covenant, and even they are not allowed to take a peek to see if it is actually there.

Language and communication have been at the forefront of the country's evolution. Today, more than 80 languages are spoken in Ethiopia by its 106 million people (which also makes Ethiopia the second most populated country in Africa). While English is the most spoken foreign language and all of the university classes are taught in English, the country has five official working languages: Amharic (which is recognized as the country's official language), Afaan Oromoo, Tigrinya, Somali, and Afar.

In the following chapters, we'll be looking at Ethiopia's biblical origins, how its empire was founded, the leaders and rulers who shaped the country's destiny, how the country's linguistics have evolved over the centuries, the important and well-documented discoveries of hominids dating back to millions of years ago and why its calendar differs from the rest of the world. We'll look at the impact these factors have had on the country's current state.

To understand the present, we must look back at the past and the history of Ethiopia to provide the answers we seek.

Chapter Two
Ancient Hominids, Husbandry, Language and Relics

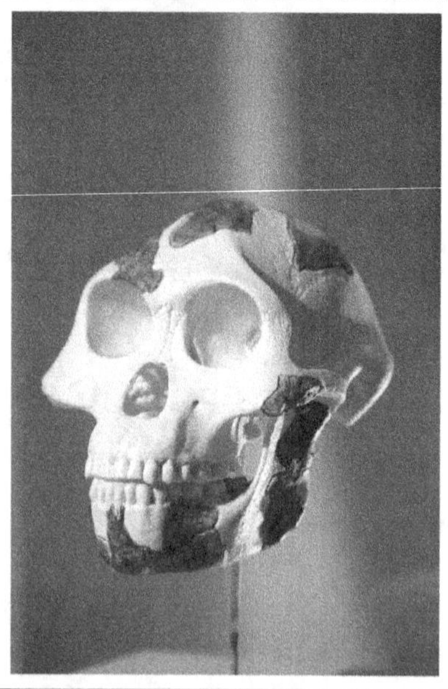

Caption: Ethiopia is home to the oldest hominid fossils in the world. Here we have Lucy, a 3.2-million-old fossil, discovered by Donald Johanson in 1974. She is one of the most complete remains ever found. Image credit: Tadias Magazine

Undeterred by legends of curses that befell Egyptian burial sites and archaeologists, Gerrard Dekker, a Dutch hydrologist, made an incredible discovery of Acheulean stone tools, estimated to be at least a million years old, in Ethiopia in 1963. Dekker's discovery indicated that hominids (a family of primates that are extinct and from which modern humans are descended) had existed in the country eons before.

It was to be the start of many similar incredible discoveries in the soil of this vibrant country. The most famous hominid remains discovered in Ethiopia is Lucy, who lived 3.2 million years ago, by Donald Johanson in 1974. Lucy is one of the most complete fossils ever found. In 1994, the famous paleontologist Tim D. White discovered a 4.4-million-year-old hominid, the oldest one to date in Ethiopia.

Tools, which look like javelins and appear to have been used by the closest ancestors of humanity, were discovered in Gademotta in 2013. These have been dated as being 195 000 years old. Proof of the Middle Ages and its grounding in Ethiopia was discovered in 2019. Projectile weapons, similar to modern-day darts, were found in Adama (ironically formerly known as Nazreth during World War II), a city in Ethiopia. Archaeologists have dated these projectile weapons as being 80 000 to 100 000 years old.

2019 proved to be a fruitful year for site diggers in Ethiopia as a team discovered a 30 000 Middle Stone Age rock shelter in the Bale Mountains of the country. Situated at 11 000 feet above sea level, this shelter is the earliest proof of the highest altitude of human occupation. Around the dawn of the new Millenium, archaeologists discovered the lost Islamic kingdom of Shoa—ruins which included a large settlement and possibly the oldest mosque on the continent. Africa being the Cradle of Mankind doesn't seem so far-fetched now, does it?

Ethiopia is considered to be the site of the emergence for the anatomically modern human. If we agree with this, the evidence to support this statement is vast. Home to several UNESCO World Heritage Sites and half of Africa's majestic mountains, Ethiopia also claims Axum, one of the oldest continuously inhabited places in Africa. From the fossils found in 1963 and 1974, it's been deduced that these hominids lived in the early Pliocene epoch and were omnivores. Their daily diet is suspected to have included plants and meat but was void of any nuts. This was most likely due to these early hominids not having similar dental features to what we modern humans have today.

Husbandry (no, we are not being sexist, this is the term for it), referring to the care, cultivation, and breeding of crops and animals, seems to have emerged in ancient Ethiopia in the latter part of the third millennium. Archaeologists were able to track the development of husbandry in the country through rock paintings of human and animal figures in the province of Hararghe. Crafting, it seems, came to Ethiopia via the Blue Nile River from Sudan.

It's fascinating to look back at how language and linguistics first evolved in ancient Ethiopia. Evidence points to early Ethiopians speaking the Hamito-Semitic or Afroasiatic languages in the third millennium BC. Linguists Charles A. Ferguson and Mauro Tosco differ in their findings and opinions about whether the Afroasiatic or Nilo-Saharan language is the origin of all Ethiopian languages spoken today. Linguistics, of course, informs the writing systems of a country. For Ethiopia, its historical writing system is the Ge'ez script. First used in the fifth and sixth centuries, the script is now mainly used by the Ethiopian and Eritrean Orthodox and Catholic Churches. While Arabic is used as the script for many Muslim followers in the country, Roman/Latin script is used for the many Cushitic, Omotic, and Nilo-Saharan languages.

First founded in 980 BC, Ethiopia is the oldest country in Africa and in 2022, is home to more than 106 million people. Since it has never been colonized, many of its cultural traditions, brought to the country from its ties to Egypt and Greece, remain largely untouched. The authenticity of its traditions, friendliness of its people, and mostly untouched natural environment and culture have continued to appeal to visitors from neighboring countries and the world.

From the fossil remains of hominids, the relics they used while they lived, the food they consumed, the languages they spoke, and the writing systems they used, Ethiopia's rich history can be traced and appreciated. Humanity is always welcome to come home to its purported origins.

Chapter Three
Links to Ancient Egypt and Greece

Caption: Ethiopians were considered exotic by the Greek people. They first appeared on Greek vases. Image credit: Egisto Sani

As the acclaimed playwright William Shakespeare once wrote: "A rose by any other name would smell as sweet," so too, is the origin of Ethiopia and its name. The Ancient Greeks were the first nation to give Ethiopia its beautiful name. First mentioned as "Aethiopia" in the revered works of Homer circa the eighth century BC, the country was claimed to be found at the east and west extremities of the world.

The Ancient Greek explorer and geographer Herodotus shared most of the detailed and earliest information about the African country Ethiopia, referring to it as "Aethiopia" in his volume of *Histories* in 440 BC. Per Herodotus's retelling, many Egyptian soldiers abandoned their country and settled alongside the tall, handsome, and long-lived men in Ethiopia. The English "Ethiopia" was first documented when the King James version of the Bible was published in 1611. It was a direct translation of the Hebrew-Greek version.

As per the country's best-known traditional tales, a Greek-speaking missionary brought Christianity to Ethiopia in the fourth century AD when he converted the ruling King Ezana of the Kingdom of Axum to his faith. Christianity thus became the state religion. Before the missionary's arrival, Ethiopia's people were split in their beliefs. Some worshiped a serpent god while others practiced Judaism. To this day, Christianity remains one of the most prominent faiths in the country. In 2019, the oldest known Christian church was discovered in the highlands of Northern Ethiopia, and it gives credit to the traditional tales told from generation to generation. To date, Christians make up 63% of the Ethiopian population in 2022.

Ethiopia's culture and politics were greatly affected by its historical links to Greece. Greek soldiers migrated to Ethiopia in great droves in the 1800s. It is believed that the Greek community was as many as 6000 people in its heyday. Today, the Ethiopian Greek community has a little over 500 members. Ethiopians were considered to be exotic to the Greek people and often depicted as black on Grecian vases, paintings, etc. The Greeks were influential members of Ethiopian high society in the early 1900s, bearing great influence on the country's emperor at the time, Haile Selassie. Ethiopians, for their part, were often cast in Greek comedies. It is from Greek artifacts that we have the lasting impression of historical Ethiopians being athletes and entertainers. A less happy legend is of Ethiopians being slaves to the Greek people. The first artistic interpretations of Ethiopians by Greek artists appear during the Hellenistic period. Sharing the Orthodox Christian religion, a sense of family, a love for good coffee, and similar tastes in entertainment ensures the ties that bind Ethiopia to Greece remain strong. In fact, many Greeks migrated to the African country after the collapse of the Greek economy in 2007.

Historically, the relations between Ethiopia and Egypt were fraught with tension, something that hasn't changed in the modern age. The first known contact between the two countries dates back to seven thousand years ago when the ancient Egyptians launched an expedition to Ethiopia's Land of Punt in the fourth century. They viewed Ethiopia as a land of great fortune. The trade relations were great between the two countries for a while, with Egyptians enjoying the gold, ebony, ivory, slaves and exotic animals that Ethiopia had in abundance.

That all changed three centuries later. Egypt and her people did not take kindly to Ethiopians invading their land. The seventh century BC ruler of the Neo-Assyrian Empire, Esarhaddon, upon conquering Egypt, deported all of the Ethiopians who lived there. While a more extensive war would ensue between Ethiopia and Egypt in the 1800s, the strife between the two countries began in the seventh century.

From a religious perspective, Egypt is responsible for bringing Islam to Ethiopia. Now the second biggest faith in Ethiopia, Islam was derived from the Al-Azhar Mosque in Cairo, Egypt. In terms of economic growth, Egypt helped to form Ethiopia's first-ever bank, the Bank of Abyssinia in 1905. Egypt controlled Ethiopia's economy until 1931 when the reigning emperor could no longer abide by having the country's bank managed by a foreign entity.

Ethiopia's greatest historic, and also its most combative, link to Egypt is that the famous Nile River, and more specifically, the Blue Nile River, has its origins in the country. The Blue Nile River springs from Lake Tana in Ethiopia. The landlocked country has benefited from being the home of this freshwater source for centuries. The Nile's water feeds the surrounding agriculture and has provided residents with livelihoods for ages.

Ethiopia started out as a melting pot of cultures. Its history informs its present and the culture thrives from being so diverse.

Chapter Four
Ethiopia's Rulers

Caption: Haile Selassie was the former Emperor of Ethiopia. Image credit: David Drissel

As famous for its discoveries of ancient hominids as its vibrant culture, Ethiopia is equally renowned for its legions of leaders and emperors. Using the style of His/her Imperial Majesty, there were 312 rulers over the course of 700 years.

By rights, the emperor was the head of state and head of government in the country. The Solomonic Dynasty, who claimed their lineage from the biblical King Solomon and the Queen of Sheba, ruled Ethiopia from the 10th century to 1974.

The first emperor of Ethiopia was Menelik I who inaugurated the Solomonic Dynasty in the 10th century. Under his rule, Ethiopia was a Jewish country. His faith was instilled by his mother, the Queen of Sheba, and further entrenched when his father King Solomon sent him home from Jerusalem with 20 Jewish soldiers to help keep his stronghold on his country. King Solomon had offered the throne of Jerusalem to his son, but Menelik I refused and chose to rule Ethiopia after his mother's death instead.

His namesake, Menelik II, reigned from 1889 to 1913. A notable ruler, Menelik II was responsible for the first signposts of modernization in Ethiopia. This emperor led his people (by uniting noblemen and regional leaders) to victory at the Battle of Adwa, the first battle between Italy and Ethiopia in 1896. As part of this historic victory, Menelik II took a stand against colonialism and ensured that Ethiopia was recognized by European leaders as being independent. He introduced Ethiopia's first modern postal service as well as brought the railway system, telephone, the motorized car and electricity to his nation. Most notably, Menelik II made the city of Addis Ababa the capital of his country. A savvy war veteran, Menelik II conquered many other cities and expanded his country's borders by bringing South Ethiopia (which until then, was mainly a Muslim country) into his realm. Through his grit, determination and success, Menelik II became a symbol of power for Black people. He is known for oppressing and enslaving minority religious figures and people and tearing down mosques in his path to victory. This famous emperor and ruler's lasting legacy is that the bountiful Ethiopia is one of the few African countries that was never colonized. He died in 1913 and was succeeded by his grandson.

The most famous emperor in Ethiopia's most recent history is Haile Selassie. The last reigning monarch of the Solomonic Dynasty, Selassie was born as Tafari Makonnen on July 23, 1892. He ascended to the Ethiopian throne on April 2, 1930, taking the name Haile Selassie I. His royal name means "Might of the Trinity." He is famous for being exiled from his birthplace and country during the Italian invasion from 1936 to 1941. Having acted as regent before his accession, Selassie had a passion for modernizing his country. Under his successful leadership, Ethiopia finally had control of its own bank and economy. He was instrumental in the creation of the Organization of African Unity, now known as the African Union, in 1963. Fighting for the freedom of his people, Selassie abolished slavery in his country and introduced Ethiopia's first written constitution in 1931.

Revered as the first messiah of the Rastafarian faith movement in Ethiopia, Selassie was a devoted Orthodox Christian and adhered to its Church's tenets. While he is viewed as one of Africa's most powerful and influential international figures (Selassie was one of the highest ranking African diplomats at the US President John F. Kennedy's funeral), many of his reforms met with some opposition from his subjects. Famine and war plagued the region of Eritrea during his reign.

Ultimately, Selassie was overthrown by the military government when they staged a revolution in 1974. Violent riots against the sudden economic inflation enforced by the emperor angered his subjects. The then-82-year-old former ruler spent his last few months imprisoned at the Grand Palace. He was assassinated on 27 August 1975.

Today, Ethiopia, a federal democratic republic, is run by a struggling government, who are constantly embroiled in conflicts with Egypt over the ownership of the Blue Nile River. The country is overpopulated, a site for gender inequality and a multitude of preventable diseases. It isn't all bleak, though, as the country also has the fastest growing economy. While most of the people living there are locally born, Ethiopia also boasts a small thriving Greek community. The country also proudly posts a female president, Sahle-Work Zewde, the first woman to hold the office.

Chapter Five

The Rise of Ethiopia During Menelik I's Reign

Caption: King Solomon meets the Queen of Sheba. Their son Menelik I would rise to become the first Solomonic Dynasty emperor. Image credit: Maître Afewerk Tekle

Information about Ethiopia's rise during the reign of its first Solomonic Dynasty Emperor Menelik I is sparse. There is more to learn about his purported mother, the Queen of Sheba and how she met his father, King Solomon, the biblical figure.

Legend has it that the Queen of Sheba traveled to Jerusalem to seek the wisdom of King Solomon that he was so famous for. The Queen of Sheba spent six months learning from King Solomon and deflecting from her worship of a sun god to believe in God. On her final night in his kingdom, legend has it, King Solomon tricked her into sharing his bed and impregnated her. The Queen of Sheba returned to Ethiopia where she bore King Solomon a son, Menelik I. The Queen of Sheba raised her son in the Jewish faith in her home country. In his 20s, the young Menelik I traveled to Jerusalem to meet his father, King Solomon. The old man attempted to persuade Menelik I to stay in Jerusalem and help him rule, but the young man was determined to return home. King Solomon then named Menelik I emperor and sent him home to Ethiopia with twenty Jewish guards to help him cement the Jewish faith as the state religion. Thus, the Solomonic Dynasty was founded and would rule, with a few interruptions here and there, for 3000 years until the final emperor, Haile Selassie, was overthrown in 1974.

Menelik I returned to Ethiopia with a gift of great importance from his father, King Solomon: the Ark of the Covenant. A sacred relic of the Israelites and one which is mentioned and lost over and over again in the Bible and the Quran, the Ark is said to be a treasure chest that contains two stone tablets of the Ten Commandments. Today, the Ethiopian

Orthodox Tewahedo Church claims to have the Ark of the Covenant in its possession in Axum. It is kept under strict surveillance and every church in Ethiopia is home to a replica. Accounts differ about whether King Solomon willingly gave the Ark of the Covenant to his son or whether Menelik I's guards smuggled the Ark out without father or son knowing about it. Either way, King Solomon lost his way after the Ark was taken and returned to worshiping his wife, the Pharaoh's daughter's false idols.

Menelik I ruled from around 950 BC. His reign is recognised worldwide as the beginning of the Solomonic Dynasty in Ethiopia. Due to the legend about his possession of the Ark of the Covenant, every Orthodox Church in the country continues to display a replica of the Ark. In November 2020 and in the midst of a global pandemic, 800 people were reportedly massacred in a fight for the Ark of the Covenant at the Church where it is housed. The victims' families were unable to bury them because their enemies would not allow them to retrieve the bodies.

Menelik I is the namesake of Menelik II who is famous for modernizing Ethiopia.

Chapter Six

The Rise of Ethiopia During the Reign of Menelik II

Caption: Emperor Menelik II led his Ethiopian army to victory against the Italian Invasion at the Battle of Adwa. Image credit: A. Davey

Menelik II, who ruled Ethiopia as its emperor from 1889 to 1913, is considered the Father of Modernization for the country. A king who chafed under the control his neighboring country Egypt held over his hometown's economy, went about setting rights to many discrepancies and admirably succeeded where his predecessors had tried and failed.

A soldier first and foremost, Menelik II is most well-known for ensuring that Ethiopia was never colonized. He led his troops against an invading Italian military force and won a decisive victory for his countrymen at the Battle of Adwa in 1896. International powers recognized the stature of Menelik II and Ethiopia by diplomatic representation at his court. To this day, Ethiopia's main source of pride remains being one of only two African countries to not be colonized. His reign is also noted for the creation of the first Cabinet of Ministers in Ethiopia. Formed to assist with the administration of the empire, these ministers were trusted and respected noblemen and retainers. Many of them served for years after the emperor's death.

Menelik II's next great task was to create the first modern bank of Ethiopia. Naming it the Bank of Abyssinia, Menelik II gave his people the freedom to manage their own finances. Fascinated by modernization since his childhood, the emperor set out to bring Western technology and administrative advances to his war-torn country. He made Addis Ababa his capital city and from here, many of the modern conveniences Ethiopia enjoys today, was born.

Menelik II introduced the first modern postal service, assisted in bringing electricity, the telephone, the telegraph, modern plumbing and the motor car to his people. In 1894, the emperor consented to the building of a railway from his capital to the French port of Djibouti. Work on the railway abruptly came to a halt when Menelik II realized that the French were trying to claim control of the line. It resumed a few years later when all parties agreed to a joint venture corporation.

A visionary as much as he was a politician, Menelik II longed to expand his empire. He fulfilled this wish by launching several wars to claim land from neighboring cities. Amongst his conquests were Oromo, Kaffa, Sidama, Wolayta, and more. He is noted too, for leading the abolishment of slavery in the mid-1890s. He achieved this by ordering the destruction of several slave markets and punishing slave traders with amputation. Menelik II eyed Russia as a great potential friend to his empire and established a diplomatic relationship with the European country in 1893.

The countries' alliances ensured that many advisers and volunteers were sent for visits to Ethiopia, and were sponsored by the Russian government. A man who spoke many languages and had a keen sense of financial matters, Menelik II was well-liked and respected by influential men around the world.

By 1898, the impressive emperor Menelik II's work was complete and once again, thriving Ethiopia had risen to its greatest modernization height at the time.

Are You Enjoying Reading?

As an independent publisher

with a tiny marketing budget

we rely on readers, like you.

If you're receiving help from this book,

would you please take a moment to write a brief review?

We really appreciate it.

Are You Enjoying Reading?

Chapter Seven

The Rise of Ethiopia During Haile Selassie's Reign

Caption: Haile Selassie was crowned as Emperor of Ethiopia in 1930.
Image credit: Maître Artiste Afewerk Tekle

As a cousin of Menelik II, Haile Selassie rose to the throne after his mother's death in 1930. Having served as regent before her death because she was a woman and was not allowed to rule in her own right, Haile Selassie had a firm grip on the kingdom. Like his cousin before him, Haile Selassie was a visionary with plenty of ideas to modernize his kingdom and strengthen his international alliances. In 1923, the then regent engineered Ethiopia's entry into the League of Nations, with the idea that it would help protect his country from aggression. A year later, he traveled to Europe and became the first Ethiopian ruler to do so.

Continuing his cousin's mission to completely abolish slavery, Haile Selassie, upon his ascension, hired key foreign advisors to assist him with his efforts. His desire to ensure the abolishment was so strong that even during his exile from Ethiopia due to the Italian Invasion, two laws were issued, in 1935 and 1936, respectively. Upon his return to his country and resuming his rule of Ethiopia, he formally included the abolishment into a written constitution in 1942. The law abolishing slavery and involuntary service was officially passed on 26 August 1942.

Under Haile Selassie's leadership, Ethiopia's economy boomed, with coffee becoming a huge commodity for the country. Traders and entrepreneurs began to penetrate the local market as Ethiopians built serviceable roads in the countryside and improved communications. Haile Selassie was particularly strict about forcing foreigners to take local partners so that he maintained control over concessions. Between 1931 and 1934, the emperor spearheaded projects that improved public services, schools, roads, hospitals, communications, and more.

Transforming the Ethiopian bank into the National Bank of Ethiopia was one of Haile Selassie's biggest achievements. He fixed the interest rate at 9% in 1921, where it had previously been set at 30%. Culturally, Haile Selassie was a pioneer too. He established the Ethiopia Scout Association in 1918 and introduced a national anthem in 1927. The dream of flight became real when the emperor welcomed airplanes to the skies of Ethiopia in 1927. Reform for offenders was a priority to the ruler, and he established a modern prison institution in 1932.

With his eye on international prominence for Ethiopia, Haile Selassie returned from his exile in the 1940s and built key relationships with major power players worldwide. Following Ethiopia's entry into the League of Nations in 1945, Haile Selassie's next big political move was to help found the Organization of African Unity (later the African Union) in 1963. Ethiopia's exportation of coffee boomed in the 1950s and sold well in markets worldwide. The revenue generated from these sales helped to centralize Ethiopia's government, improve communications and facilitated an overhaul of the country's educational system so that it matched the one Western country were employing.

Haile Selassie's rule is remembered as one of political, economic, and cultural revolution for Ethiopia. Many of the freedoms the country's people enjoy today can be traced back to his reign.

Chapter Eight
The Fall of Ethiopia During Menelik I's Reign

Caption: The Ark of the Covenant came to Ethiopia with Menelik I after his visit to his father King Solomon in Jerusalem. Image credit: Blake Patterson

Not much has been recorded about the downfall of the first Solomonic Dynasty emperor's reign. What we know comes from biblical texts and legend. A few things are quite clear around the legacy of Menelik I: superstition dogged his short-lived reign, and he did not ultimately succeed in maintaining the Jewish faith in Ethiopia, thus resulting in a fall for the country.

Superstition cast a shadow:

King Solomon wanted to give his throne to Menelik I, since he was technically the King's first-born son, but the young man refused the honor. King Solomon then offered to give Menelik I a replica of the original Ark of the Covenant. There are differing accounts about whether King Solomon gifted the real Ark of the Covenant to his son Menelik I or whether the very guards he charged with protecting his desired heir stole the priceless religious relic from his palace. If we follow the legend that Menelik I's new men stole the Ark of the Covenant, it is said that nothing befell their journey back to Ethiopia, despite the many powerful traits the Ark was said to possess. Menelik I reasoned that since nothing had happened, it meant the artifact was meant to be with him.

His father, King Solomon, on the other hand, faltered in his faith to his one true God and turned instead to his wife, the Pharaoh's daughter's false idols. He had sent soldiers to hunt down his son and his treacherous guards but could not find any trace of them, thus lending credit to the claim that the Ark had chosen to hide its true owner, Menelik I.

A short-lived reign and obscurity:

In comparison to many of his descendants, Menelik I ruled for a very short time. With just 25 years to his credit, it is believed that Menelik I did not do much in terms of the advancement of Ethiopia and her people. Additionally, information about Menelik I is sparse in all three major religious tomes: the Bible, the Quran and the Torah. This is in direct contrast to his mother, the Queen of Sheba, for which all three religions have similar origin stories, albeit with different names for the Queen.

His religion did not last:

While Menelik I tried to have his people fall under the law of Moses, he ultimately failed to keep it going. Soon, Orthodox Christianity and Islam would be brought to Ethiopia through Greek and Egyptian envoys. The mystique around the Ark of the Covenant has led to many violent riots, the most recent being in 2020, when 800 people were killed at an Orthodox Christian Church in the pursuit of finding it and claiming it as their own.

The mystique that surrounds Menelik I, his parents King Solomon and the Queen of Sheba as well as the Ark of the Covenant remains part of Ethiopia's history to this day. What remains of their story is told through panels, religious text and the age-old word of mouth marketing—stories told from generation to generation.

Chapter Nine
The Fall of Ethiopia During the Reign of Menelik II

Caption: Menelik II's successful victory at the Battle of Adwa is well remembered but his grab for power was not. Image credit: A. Davey

As one of the longer reigning emperors, Menelik II is renowned for keeping Ethiopia independent and bringing technological advances to his country. He is equally famous for alienating his people, his grab for power and his failing health that left Ethiopia exposed and vulnerable.

The alienation of southern citizens:

Menelik II's expansion into the South of Ethiopia was initially met with great excitement. Bringing all of Ethiopia together under one rule seemed like cause for celebration, but it was short-lived. The ruler introduced a system of land rights in North Ethiopia that was vastly different from other African countries at the time. In giving the noblemen the same rights, and often more than ordinary citizens who owned their land through their birthright, Menelik II created a division between his people that would fester and lead to the downfall of his empire seventy years later.

Meanwhile, the South of the country belonged to the emperor. Here, he divided his land between his appointments to office and to his loyal soldiers. Additionally, he gave his high ranking officials and soldiers rights that essentially made the indigenous people of the South tenants to these officers. Thus, these indigenous people became aliens on the land they used to own and would remain that way.

Menelik II's grab for international power:

The emperor is famous for his successful victory at the Battle of Adwa, saving Ethiopia's independence against an Italian Invasion. What historians often forget to mention is that the Italians were only able to get a toehold into Ethiopia because Menelik II initially invited them in by negotiating the Treaty of Wuchale in 1889. Relations soured between Ethiopia and Italy when the latter overextended its expansion and reach.

Despite his successful Battle of Adwa, Menelik II and Ethiopia was set upon by Britain, France, and Italy when the three countries aligned their interests to have a stronger hold on the empire in the later 1890s. Additionally, Menelik II was fighting off Russia, Germany and the Ottoman Empire's interest in Ethiopia. By playing all of these major international powers off against each other, Menelik II successfully managed to maintain his country's borders without making any great concessions.

Menelik II's endless hunger for power led to him teaming up with France to invade Sudan in 1898. In 1904, he and Ethiopia helped the British to put down a Somalian rebellion.

Menelik II's failing health left Ethiopia exposed:

In May 1906, Menelik II suffered a debilitating stroke. His until-then iron will and firm grip on power began slipping and his foes took this opportunity to avoid conflict in the Ethiopian empire. Britain, France, and Italy signed the Tripartite Treaty which allowed them each to continue their trade in their respective regions of Ethiopia and maintain the status quo. In response to his political influence waning, Menelik II established a Council of Ministers in 1907 to help manage the country. It would prove to be a bad decision since these same ministers would ultimately end up

fighting for control of the country after Menelik II's death.

Chapter Ten
The Fall of Ethiopia During Haile Selassie's Reign

Caption: Pictured above is a statue of Haile Selassie, the last emperor of Ethiopia. Image credit: Jay Galvin

The nearly 45-year rule of the last emperor of Ethiopia, Haile Selassie, was one of the country's most impressive and divisive ones. As a ruler,

Haile Selassie's fall, and that of Ethiopia, led to the abolishment of the monarchy altogether in 1974.

His authoritarian rule:

Like his cousin Menelik II before him, Haile Selassie liked to be in control. It was his way or no way, and it would eventually mean his end. He ruled with an iron fist and was renowned for violently putting down any rebellion against his rule. He stands accused of dragging his feet on the abolishment of slavery, a law which only came to pass in 1942, because the slave trade benefited him when need be. The first modern constitution he introduced in 1955 left most of the country's power firmly in Haile Selassie and his descendants' hands.

His willful ignorance:

While Haile Selassie's rule is mostly remembered as a time of prosperity for Ethiopia, there are some blights on his good name. The last Solomonic Dynasty Emperor willfully ignored the widespread famine in huge parts of his country from 1972 to 1975. A human rights group has accused the leader of ignoring and trying to cover up the starvation and death of an estimated 200 000 of Ethiopia's residents. Reports have it that Haile Selassie spent more than $35 million on his eightieth birthday celebrations in 1973, while the people of Ethiopia were starving. The emperor ate his cake and had it too while his people suffered horribly.

His hubris:

Haile Selassie's ego was a huge problem and marred his rule of Ethiopia. His acceptance of being declared a god by the Rastafarian people was not because he believed in their declaration or because he held a great love for them. Haile Selassie is believed to have only granted some 1000 Rastafarian people land in his country because it was a good public relations move. Today, there are only 400 Rastafarians living in their stronghold in Ethiopia, and they are largely separated from the rest of the country, who firmly follow either the Orthodox Christianity or Islamic faiths.

The egotistic Haile Selassie took credit for others' work. During the Italian occupation in the late 1930s and early 1940s, while Haile Selassie was exiled, it was Lorenzo Taezaz, an Eritrean, who arranged the uprising of Ethiopians against the Italians. Yet, it is Haile Selassie who is remembered for conquering the Italians and reclaiming Ethiopia's independence. Similarly, the legendary speech Haile Selassie delivered in 1936 to the League of Nations, is reported to have been written by Taezaz.

Haile Selassie, the last Emperor of Ethiopia, was overthrown by a military force in 1974. His people had grown weary of his dictatorship, his advancement of his own people above the countrymen and his negligence. While the country is now run by elected public servants, Ethiopia remains a land of famine, war and poverty. Haile Selassie's legacy was the fall of Ethiopia.

Chapter Eleven

The Aftermath of the Fall of Ethiopia

In the aftermath of the many rises and falls of Ethiopia, her people are diverse and celebrate their differences. Image credit: Wikimedia

Ethiopia, the landlocked African country, has been ruled by emperors, the military and a parliament for more than 3000 years. The aftermath of the country's various rises and falls are still felt today.

The Ethiopian people remain divided by religion, famine, war and strife. Menelik I, the famous son of the biblical King Solomon and Queen of Sheba worked hard to bring Judaism to his home country but left behind a legacy of a religious rift instead. In the 21st century, wars and massacres continue to be held and done in the name of religious superiority. Menelik I's legendary possession of the Ark of the Covenant and housing it in a small church in the Northern parts of his country continue to lead to the spilling of blood.

His namesake Menelik II's reign was hailed as an age of revolution but his legacy too, led to the fall of Ethiopia. By gifting land and wealth to his own descendants, soldiers and noblemen, he deprived the indigenous people of their birthrights. Ethiopia's people remain divided by economic status and land ownership. While his political power plays ensured Ethiopia was seen as an international powerhouse, it also left the country vulnerable to invasions, occupations, and endless violence.

His successor and kinsman Haile Selassie fared no better. While outwardly and internationally inclined, he was seen as a champion for the African people and a prime example of a politically savvy statesman, his countrymen revile him as a harsh dictator whose costly mistakes they are still living with generations later. Ethiopia, whilst celebrated as the homeland of coffee worldwide and a melting pot of cultures, remains one of the poorest countries in the world. Even with a democratically elected government, Ethiopia and her people remain hungry and are often at blood shedding war with each other and their neighboring countries.

The aftermath of the many rises and falls of this country does include some positive things as well. Ethiopia remains one of only two African countries that has never been colonized. It continues to be recognized for its independence. It is famous for being the birthplace of coffee, a beloved global beverage. By allowing foreign envoys into its borders, Ethiopian leaders brought technology, culture and infrastructure to their beloved country. Groundbreaking historical and scientific discoveries have been made in this beautiful land. Ethiopia was a pioneer of bringing electricity, railroads and trade to Africa. As the oldest African country, Ethiopia is the sprawling home to a diverse population who mostly live in relative peace together, practicing major religion in relative harmony and speak over 80 different languages and dialects. This celebrated diversity extends to music too as Ethiopia is where Ethio-jazz was born, thanks to musician Mulatu Astatke adding the five notes of Ethiopian music to the 12 notes of jazz in the 1970s.

For all of its often-violent history, Ethiopia has emerged as home to 106 million people and a must-visit location for millions of visitors in our vast world. To draw on its national anthem, "March Forward, Dear Mother Ethiopia."

Chapter Twelve

Conclusion

Looking back at the history of Ethiopia, it would be all too easy to conclude that its violent wars, religious differences and combative factions have left the country a war-torn, barren land. However, this is not the case. For all of their many faults, each ruling emperor served the empire well, ensuring that Ethiopia, their beautiful motherland, advanced in modernization, faith, agriculture and infrastructure. As Africa's oldest country, Ethiopia stands out as an example of what the fight for independence, the meshing of people of various cultures and the thirst for knowledge can be achieved by the visionary mindsets of her leaders.

Home to the origin of the famous Nile River, bountiful Ethiopia truly is the motherland. Not only does she sustain 106 million people, hers is the land of the largest population of livestock. Her rich soil has produced some of history's greatest discoveries (amongst them, the oldest most complete fossil of a hominid, Lucy) and has produced the world's most treasured bean—coffee. Known as being the top producer of honey in Africa, Ethiopia's contributions to the global trade remains a highlight. Gold medalists, including the impressive world-record-breaking long-distance runner Haile Gebrselassie, were born, raised and trained to be the finest at their sport on Ethiopia's vast lands.

Religion has been a mainstay of Ethiopia since the empire's formation. From Menelik I's introduction of Judaism to the advent of Orthodox Christianity by a Greek missionary and Menelik II bringing Islam into the country through the conquering of South Ethiopia and its Muslim people, Ethiopia now houses 80 different ethnic groups, languages, cultures and dialects. Tourists to the country can get a taste of the world in the confines of Ethiopia. Home to a small contingent of both Greeks and Rastafarians, Ethiopia has welcomed plenty of foreigners to her land. With her mostly vegetarian-based cuisine, the country is already a favorite amongst eco-conscious visitors. Music is another of Ethiopia's specialties—it is here where the fusion genre Ethio-jazz was born in the 1970s.

While she remains one of the poorest countries in the world, Ethiopia also has the fastest growing economy in East Africa and globally. Her future, with seeds sown by her many notable leaders, looks bright as the country has the second largest hydropower potential in Africa. As a pioneer of bringing electricity, railroads, the telephone, banks and motor cars to the continent, Ethiopia has always led the charge. Hope prevails that with the correct leadership from her democratically elected government, Ethiopia can once again be a forward-thinking nation and inspiration to the rest of Africa and the world.

As former President of South Africa and a renowned global icon Nelson Mandela once said: "Ethiopia always has a special place in my imagination and the prospect of visiting Ethiopia attracted me more strongly than a trip to France, England, and America combined. I felt I would be visiting my own genesis, unearthing the roots of what made me an African." Let us all strive to unearth our roots in Mother Ethiopia.

Chapter Thirteen

Discussion Question

The Solomonic Dynasty claims to be descended from the biblical King Solomon and Queen of Sheba. With scriptures being passed down orally for generations and only printed in the 1600s, how sure are we that this is true? How would we be able to prove or disprove this theory?

Discussion Question

The conflict with Egypt over the Nile River has been raging on for years. Currently, Egypt is angry about the dam Ethiopia has built to retain their share of the water. Do you think Egypt is entitled to more water? If so, why?

Discussion Question

Ethiopia has never been colonized. This is in part due to Menelik II and the last emperor who successfully took back the country from the Italians. Why do you think Ethiopia succeeded where other countries did not?

Discussion Question

Despite so many important scientific and historical discoveries made in Ethiopia, it remains one of the poorest countries in the world. Why do you think this is? How could the situation be rectified?

Discussion Question

In many ways, Ethiopia was always at the forefront of technology in centuries gone by. This seems to not be the case any longer. Can the country reclaim its spot in the technology-first world or not?

Discussion Question

If the Greeks had not brought Christianity to Ethiopia, it may still have been a Jewish nation by the time Islam arrived. This would no doubt have turned the country into a second Palestine vs Jerusalem. How do you think that would have impacted its economic and political growth?

Discussion Question

With its many historical discoveries, Ethiopia is sitting on a potential goldmine. It already draws plenty of curious visitors. Should the government be hiking up tourist visa prices? Is it ethical to do so?

Discussion Question

Ethiopia has a rich history and culture. Looking back, there were many contributing factors to this. What or who stood out to you the most, and why?

Chapter Fourteen
Quiz Question

1. **. True or False:** Menelik II was a pioneer of many of Ethiopia's modern facilities. He is renowned for bringing electricity, the motorized car and telephone to the country. He also brought the Internet to Ethiopia.

2. **True or False:** Ethiopia is a sprawling country in Africa. Its borders have expanded exponentially over the centuries. Menelik II brought South Ethiopia into the fold during his reign.

3. **True or False:** Religion has always been at the heart of Ethiopia's rule. Orthodox Christianity and Islam are the two dominating religions in the present. Before adopting Christianity as the state religion, Ethiopians were Jewish.

4. **True or False:** A country known for its agricultural properties; Ethiopia has the Blue Nile River running through it. The country is the origin of one of the world's most beloved beverages. Ethiopia is the birthplace of tea.

5. **True or False:** The Solomonic Dynasty ruled Ethiopia for over 3000 years. Some of the most notable emperors include Haile Selassie, Menelik I and Menelik II. There have been 312 emperors in Ethiopia.

6. **True or False:** A melting pot of cultures and people, Ethiopia is home to over 106 million residents. In addition to having many types of writing systems, the Ethiopians also speak many languages. There are over 80 different languages spoken in the country.

7. **True or False:** Ethiopia has fought hard for its independence. It is one of only two countries to never be colonized. This was achieved by defeating Italy.

8. **True or False:** The monarchy was abolished in 1974. Since then, a federal democratic republic has been established. Today, the country has a female president.

Quiz Answer

1. False: Menelik II died in 1913, more than six decades before the advent of the Internet.

2. True

3. True

4. False: It is the birthplace of coffee.

5. True

6. True

7. True

8. True

Bonus Downloads

*Get Free Books with **<u>Any Purchase</u>** History Shorts*

Every purchase comes with a FREE download!

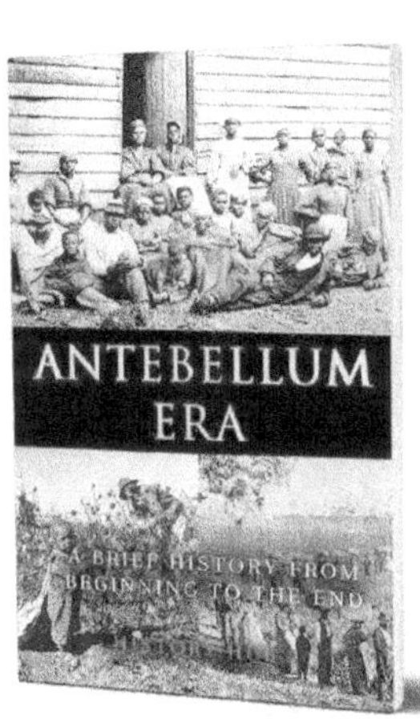